D1566847

What is the Voice?

SonLight Education Ministry
United States of America

A Suggested Daily Schedule

(Adapt this schedule to your family needs.)

5:00 a.m.   Arise–Personal Worship

6:00 a.m.   Family Worship and Bible Class–With Father

7:00 a.m.   Breakfast

8:00 a.m.   Practical Arts*–Domestic Activities
                                  Agriculture
                                  Industrial Arts
                                  (especially those related to
                                  the School Lessons)

10:00 a.m.   School Lessons
                                  (Take a break for some physical exercise
                                  during this time slot.)

12:00 p.m.   Dinner Preparations
                                  (Health class could be included at this time
                                  or a continued story.)

1:00 p.m.   Dinner

2:00 p.m.   Practical Arts* or Fine Arts
                                  (Music and Crafts)
                                  (especially those related to
                                  the School Lessons)

5:00 p.m.   Supper

6:00 p.m.   Family Worship–Father
                                  (Could do History Class)

7:00 p.m.   Personal time with God–Bed Preparation

8:00 p.m.   Bed

*Daily nature walk can be in morning or afternoon.

The Desire of All Nations

This book is a part of a curriculum that is built upon the life of Christ entitled, "The Desire of All Nations," for grades 2-8. Any of the books in this curriculum can be used by themselves or as an entire program.

INFORMATION ABOUT THE 2-8 GRADE PROGRAM

Multi-level

This program is written on a multi-level. That means that each booklet has material for grades 2-8. This is so the whole family in these grades may work from the same books. It is difficult for a busy mother to have 2 or more children and each have a different set of books. Remember, the Bible is written for all ages.

The Bible—the Primary Textbook

The books in this program are designed to teach the parent and the student how to learn academic subjects by using the Bible as a primary textbook.

The Desire of Ages

The Desire of Ages by Ellen G. White is used as a textbook to go with the Bible. This focuses on the early life of Christ, when He was a child. Children relate best to Christ as a child and youth.

Lesson Numbers

The big number in the top right corner on the cover of this book is the Lesson Number and corresponds with the chapter number in the book *The Desire of Ages*. For example, Lesson 1 in the school program will go along with chapter 1 in *The Desire of Ages*. Usually each family starts at the beginning with Lesson 1. Most children have not had a true Bible program, therefore they need the foundation built. If there is academic material that they have already covered, they do the Bible part and review then pass quickly on.

Seven Academic Subjects

There are seven academic subjects in this program—Health, Mathematics, Music, Science–Nature, History/Geography/Prophecy, Language, Voice–Speech.

Language Program

A good, solid language program is recommended to be used along with the SonLight materials.

The Riggs Institute has a multi-sensory teaching method that accommodates every child's unique learning style. Their program is called *Writing and Spelling Road to Reading and Thinking*. Order by calling (800) 200-4840 or visit www.riggsinst.org. (Disclaimer: SonLight does not endorse the reading books recommended in the Riggs' program.)

Another option which you might find more user friendly and is similar to the Riggs program but from a Christian perspective is *Spell to Write and Read* by Wanda Sanseri. To order, call Wanda Sanseri at (503) 654-2300 or visit https://www.bhibooks.net/swr.html

"God With Us"
Lesson 1 – Love

The following books are those you will need for this lesson.
All of these can be obtained from www.sonlighteducation.com

The Rainbow Covenant – Study the spiritual meaning of colors and make your own rainbow book.

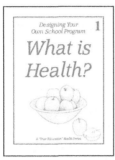

Health
What is Health?

Math
What is Mathematics?

Music
What is Music?

Science/Nature
What is Nature?

A Casket – Coloring book and story. Learn how to treat the gems of the Bible.

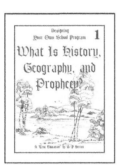

H/G/P
What is History, Geography and Prophecy?

Language
What is Language?

Speech/Voice
What is the Voice?

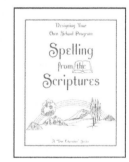

Spelling from the Scriptures

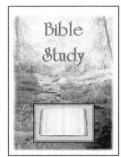

Bible Study – Learn how to study the Bible and helpful use tools.

Bible
The Desire of all Nations I
Teacher Study Guide

Student Study Guide

Bible Lesson Study Guide

Memory Verses
The Desire of all Nations I
Scripture Songs Book

and MP3 files

Our Nature Study Book – Your personal nature journal.

Outline of "The Desire of all Nations" Lesson 1

READ THIS BEFORE BEGINNING

Cover the Teacher's Section of each school book before beginning that subject.

It is best to cover only a few concepts at once and understand them well and not run a marathon with a young person's mind.

If this outline moves to fast for you SLOW down. Teach one idea and teach it well!

This school program is not a race with time, rather it is an experience with God.

The parents are to represent their Father in Heaven before the children—students.

Together learn about the Character Qualities and help one another in a godly manner to reach the finish line together.

INSTRUCTIONS

Bible	Health	Math	Music	Nature	H/G/P	Language	Voice
Week 1 / Month 1 / Lesson 1 / Day 1 Family Morning Worship *Covenant Notebook* (1) Music, Prayer, MV (2) Read pages 1-2 in the "Covenant Notebook" and discuss. (3) Sometime during the day take a nature walk looking for rainbows. (4) Begin finding pictures of complete rainbows to put into the plastic sheets behind the "Rainbows" page. Read and discuss the "Rainbows" page.	Use these songs during this week, "All Things Bright & Beautiful," "This is My Father's World," and "We Shall Know." Find this music in *Christ in Song* book which is included in these materials under the title "Song Books."						
Day 2 (1) Music, Prayer, MV (2) Read page 3 in the "Covenant Notebook" and discuss. (Also use page 7)	Lay out Lesson 1 of the School Program showing the front covers of each book, *What is Health?, What is Mathematics?, What is Music?, What is Nature?,*	*What is H/G/P?, What is Language?, and What is Voice?.* Each book will have a color cover of one of the colors of the rainbow. Place them in order as the rainbow colors	deomonstrate in a picture. Refer to page 7 of the *Covenant Notebook* to see what each color means and how it relates to the subject that bears that color.	(Examples: Health = Christ sacrificed His body on the cross for you. Mathematics = Deals in numbers saved and lost.	Music = Right music can turn our thoughts from things of this world to Divinity. Nature = Right growth in character.	H/G/P = The history of obedience and disobedience; geography of lands where the gospel is to be spread; prophecy telling us the future of those keeping the law.	Language and Voice = How God's royal people should write, speak, and act to prepare for His kingdom.

Bible	Health	Math	Music	Nature	H/G/P	Language	Voice

(3) Sometime during the day take a nature walk looking for rainbows.

(4) Begin finding pictures of complete rainbows to put into the plastic sheets behind the "Rainbows" page. Read and discuss the "Rainbows" page.

Day 3-4

(1) Music, Prayer, MV

(2) Read pages 4-9 in the "Covenant Notebook" and discuss.

(3) Sometime during the day take a nature walk looking for white items (or the color pages).

(4) Begin finding pictures of white things in nature to put into the plastic sheets behind the "White" page. Read and discuss the "White" page.

Day 5

Review what you have learned.

INSTRUCTIONS

Once the white page is completed then move on to the red page and so forth, always finding things from nature for your pictures. And on your nature walks fine the color you are currently working on. Do not look for man made things! Before going on the nature walk each day, read and discuss the information in the color section.

After day 5, and reviewing only what you have learned to that point, plan only to work on the *Covenant Notebook* one day a week until that book is finished (Use time in the afternoon and not during the regular school hours). However, do not forget to review the *Covenant Notebook* when you deem it necessary, and if you should find a new picture for it, stop and put it into *Covenant Notebook*. It gives you an opportunity to review lessons with the children.

Lesson 12 of Nature in this series is about the rainbow and would be a wonderful time to make a recommitment to God.

This *Covenant Notebook* is to prepare you for the 2-8 School Lessons. On week 2 begin the School Lessons.

Bible	Health	Math	Music	Nature	H/G/P	Language	Voice

START THE 2-8 PROGRAM, "The Desire Of All Nations."

Bible	Health	Math	Language
Week 2 Lesson 1			
Day 1 "God With Us" (1) Music ("O Come, O come, Immanuel," "I Love Thee," "Thou didst Leave Thy Throne"), Prayer, MV (Mt 1:21) (2) Read and discuss Ge 3:14-15; 12:1-3. Discuss the Character Quality.	**Day 1** *What Is Health?* (1) Open Bibles and read II Sa 20:9. (2) Read or tell information. Do pages 1-17 or what you can cover. Discuss.	**Day 1** *What Is Math...?* (1) Open Bibles and read Mt 11:29. (2) Read or tell information. Do pages 1-8 or what you can cover. Discuss.	**Day 1** *Writing and Spelling Road to Reading and Thinking (WSRRT)* (1) Do your daily assignments for *WSRRT*. If you are still working on this program continue until you finish at least the 2nd teacher's notebook.

INSTRUCTIONS

If you are still using the *Family Bible Lessons* do them for one of your worships each day and use *The Desire of all Nations* for the other worship each day.

These are the items you will need for worship for *The Desire of all Nations* Bible program: Old King James Bible (**NOT** the New King James Bible)
    "*The Desire of all Nations,*" Volume 1, Study Guide for the
        KJV Bible Lessons
The Desire of all Nations Teacher and Student Study Guides #1
    (Chapters from *The Desire of Ages* Bible text book)
The Desire of all Nations Song Book #1 and CD Music #1
    for Memory Verses
Christ in Song Song Book #1, 2, 3, 4

These are the items you will need for class time:

*What is Health?; What is Mathematics?; What is Music?;
What is Nature?; What is H/G/P?; What is Language?; and
What is Voice?.*
Our Nature Study Book   "The Casket" Story & Coloring Book
Bible Study
Road Map and Route Catalogue

Voice	Language	H/G/P	Nature	Music	Math	Health	Bible
	Day 2 *Writing and Spelling Road to Reading and Thinking* (1) Do your daily assignments for *WSRRT*.				**Day 2** *What Is Math…?* (1) Open Bibles and read Luke 6:38; Is 40:12; Ps 147:4; Is 40:26; Job 28:25. (2) Read or tell information. Do pages 9-22 or what you can cover. Discuss. **END**	**Day 2** *What Is Health?* (1) Open Bibles and read I Co 12:23. (2) Read or tell information. Do pages 18-26 or what you can cover. Discuss.	**Day 2** "God With Us" (1) Music ("O Come, O Come, Immanuel," "I Love Thee," "Thou didst Leave Thy Throne"), Prayer, MV (Mt 1:21; Jn 8:28) (2) Read and discuss Gal 3:16; Ge 49:10; De 18:17-19; II Sam 7:12-17.
	Day 3 *Writing and Spelling Road to Reading and Thinking* (1) Do your daily assignments for *WSRRT*.			**Day 3** *What Is Music?* (1) Open Bibles and read Zeph 3:17. (2) Read or tell information. Do pages 1-6 or what you can cover. Discuss.		**Day 3** *What Is Health?* (1) Open Bibles and read Pr 26:2. (2) Read or tell information. Do pages 27-35 or what you can cover. Discuss.	**Day 3** "God With Us" (1) Music, Prayer, MV (Mt 1:21; Jn 8:28) (2) Read and discuss Ez 21:25-27; Lu 1:32; Isa 9:6-7.
	Day 4 *Writing and Spelling Road to Reading and Thinking* (1) Do your daily assignments for *WSRRT*.			**Day 4** *What Is Music?* (1) Open Bibles and read Re 14:2-3. (2) Read or tell information. Do pages 7-17 or what you can cover. Discuss.	**Day 4** *What Is Math…?* (1) Review.	**Day 4** *What Is Health?* (1) Review pages 1-35.	**Day 4** "God With Us" (1) Review what you have already covered.
	Day 5 Review			**Day 5**	**Day 5**	**Day 5**	**Day 5**

Find practical applications from your textbooks you have thus far used this week. You will find them listed under "**Reinforce**." Choose and use today.

Bible	Health	Math	Music	Nature	H/G/P	Language	Voice
Week 3 Lesson 1 **Day 1** "God With Us" (1) Music, Prayer, MV (Mt 1:21; Jn 8:28) (2) Read and discuss Ps 45:1-8; 72:1-11; Is 53.	**Day 1** *What Is Health?* (1) Open Bibles and read James 5:14. (2) Read or tell information. Do pages 36-39 or what you can cover. Discuss.		**Day 1** *What Is Music?* (1) Open Bibles and read I Ki 19:12. (2) Read or tell information. Do pages 18-30 or what you can cover. Discuss.			**Day 1** *Writing and Spelling Road to Reading and Thinking* (1) Do your daily assignments for *WSRRT.*	
Day 2 "God With Us" (1) Music, Prayer, MV (Mt 1:21; Jn 8:28; Jn 8:50) (2) Read and discuss Zec 12:10; Jn 14:9; Mt 1:23; Jn 1:1-4.	**Day 2** *What Is Health?* (1) Open Bibles and read De 34:7. (2) Read or tell information. Do pages 40-44 or what you can cover. Discuss.		**Day 2** *What Is Music?* (1) Open Bibles and read I Chr 13:8. (2) Read or tell information. Do pages 31-52 or what you can cover. Discuss. END			**Day 2** *Writing and Spelling Road to Reading and Thinking* (1) Do your daily assignments for *WSRRT.*	
Day 3 "God With Us" (1) Music, Prayer, MV (Mt 1:21; Jn 8:28; Jn 8:50; Phil 2:5-11) (2) Read and discuss *The Desire of Ages* 19-20:0.	**Day 3** *What Is Health?* (1) Open Bibles and read Ez 33:11. (2) Read or tell information. Do pages 45-53 or what you can cover. Discuss.			**Day 3** *What Is Nature?* (1) Open Bibles and read Ro 13:10. (2) Read or tell information. Do pages 1-11 or what you can cover. Discuss.		**Day 3** *Writing and Spelling Road to Reading and Thinking* (1) Do your daily assignments for *WSRRT.*	

Bible	Health	Math	Music	Nature	H/G/P	Language	Voice
Day 4 "God With Us" (1) Music, Prayer, MV (Mt 1:21; Jn 8:28; Jn 8:50; Phil 2:5-11) (2) Read and discuss *The Desire of Ages* 20:2-21:0.	**Day 4** *What Is Health?* (1) Open Bibles and read De 7:15; De 32:46; and Pr 4:20, 22. (2) Read or tell information. Do pages 54-60 or what you can cover. Discuss.			**Day 4** *What Is Nature?* (1) Open Bibles and read Ps 40:5; Ps 111:4. (2) Read or tell information. Do pages 12-17 or what you can cover. Discuss.		**Day 4** *Writing and Spelling Road to Reading and Thinking* (1) Do your daily assignments for *WSRRT*.	
Day 5 "God With Us" (1) Review.	**Day 5** *What Is Health?* (1) Review pages 1-60.	**Day 5** *What Is Math...?* (1) Review.	**Day 5** *What Is Music?* (1) Review.	**Day 5** *What Is Nature?* (1) Review pages 1-17.		**Day 5** *Writing and Spelling Road to Reading and Thinking* (1) Do your daily assignments for *WSRRT*.	
Week 4 Lesson 1 **Day 1** "God With Us" (1) Music, Prayer, MV (Mt 1:21; Jn 8:28; Jn 8:50; Phil 2:5-11) (2) Read and discuss *The Desire of Ages* 21:1-2.	**Day 1** *What Is Health?* (1) Open Bibles and read De 7:15; De 32:46; and Pr 4:20, 22. (2) Read the story. Do pages 61-80. Discuss.			**Day 1** *What Is Nature?* (1) Open Bibles and read Job 12:7-8. (2) Read or tell information. Do pages 18-23 or what you can cover. Discuss.		**Day 1** *Writing and Spelling Road to Reading and Thinking* (1) Do your daily assignments for *WSRRT*.	
Day 2 "God With Us" (1) Music, Prayer, MV (Mt 1:21; Jn 8:28; Jn 8:50; Phil 2:5-11) (2) Read and discuss *The Desire of Ages* 21:3-22:1.	**Day 2** *What Is Health* (1) Open Bibles and review De 7:15; De 32:46; and Pr 4:20, 22. (2) Do pages 81-86. Discuss. **END**			**Day 2** *What Is Nature?* (1) Open Bibles and read Ps 143:5. (2) Read or tell information. Do pages 24-30 or what you can cover. **END**		**Day 2** *WSRRT* (1) Do your daily assignments for *WSRRT*. Continue the *WSRRT* but add the Language lessons in whenever it is time to do them. **This will not be repeated.**	

Bible	Health	Math	Music	Nature	H/G/P	Language	Voice
Day 3 "God With Us" (1) Music, Prayer, MV (Mt 1:21; Jn 8:28; Jn 8:50; Phil 2:5-11) (2) Read and discuss *The Desire of Ages* 21:3-22:3.					**Day 3** *What Is H/G/P?* (1) Open Bibles and read He 1:10. (2) Read or tell information. Do pages 1-6 or what you can cover. Discuss. Choose a good mission book to begin reading as a family.	**Day 3** *What Is Language?* (1) Open Bibles and read Col 3:16. (2) Read or tell information. Do pages 1-10 or what you can cover + *WSRRT*. Discuss.	
Day 4 "God With Us" (1) Music, Prayer, MV (Mt 1:21; Jn 8:28; Jn 8:50; Phil 2:5-11) (2) Read and discuss *The Desire of Ages* 21:3-22:3.					**Day 4** *What Is H/G/P?* (1) Open Bibles and read Ps 119:105 & He 13:1. (2) Read or tell information. Do pages 7-14. Discuss.	**Day 4** *What Is Language?* (1) Open Bibles and read Pr 25:11. (2) Read or tell information. Do pages 11-17 + *WSRRT*. Discuss.	**Day 4** *What Is Voice?* (1) Open Bibles and read Ps 105:2. (2) Read or tell information. Do pages 1-4 Discuss.
Day 5 "God With Us" (1) Review. (2) Read and discuss *The Desire of Ages* 22:4-24:1.	**Day 5** *What Is Health?* (1) Review	**Day 5** *What Is Math....?* (1) Review.	**Day 5** *What Is Music?* (1) Review.	**Day 5** *What Is Nature?* (1) Review.	**Day 5** *What Is H/G/P?* (1) Review pages 1-14.	**Day 5** *What Is Language?* (1) Review pages 1-17.	**Day 5** *What Is Voice?* (1) Review pages 1-4.
		If there is any information that the student should know and does not—REVIEW.				Do your daily assignments for *WSRRT*.	
Week 1 (5) Lesson 1 **Day 1** "God With Us" (1) Music, Prayer, MV. (2) Read and discuss *The Desire of Ages* 24:2-26:3.	Month 2				**Day 1** *What Is H/G/P?* (1) Open Bibles and read Jer 10:12. (2) Read or tell information. Do pages 15-25Aa or what you can cover. Discuss.	**Day 1** *What Is Language?* (1) Open Bibles and read Jn 1:1. (2) Read or tell information. Do pages 18-22 or what you can cover. Discuss. **END**	**Day 1** *What Is Voice?* (1) Open Bibles and read Ps 32:2. (2) Read or tell information. Do pages 5-8. Discuss. **END**

Bible	Health	Math	Music	Nature	H/G/P	Language	Voice
Day 2 "God With Us" (1) Music, Prayer, MV. (2) Expand or review any part of the lesson. (Could use section about William Miller in H/G/P.) **Day 3** "God With Us" (1) Music, Prayer, MV. (2) Expand or review any part of the lesson. (Could use the section in H/G/P, "The Schools of the Prophets.") **Day 4** "God With Us" (1) Music, Prayer, MV. (2) Expand or review any part of the lesson. (Could explain why the Apocrypha books are not included in Bible.) **END**					**Day 2** *What Is H/G/P?* (1) Open Bibles and read II Pe 1:21. (2) Read or tell information. Do pages 26-47 or what you can cover. Discuss. (Story about "William Miller" may take longer.) **Day 3** *What Is H/G/P?* (1) Open Bibles and read Ja 3:17 & Pr 9:10. (2) Read or tell information. Do pages 48-65 or what you can cover. Discuss. **Day 4** *What Is H/G/P?* (1) Open Bibles and read Ex 17:14 & Ge 5:22. (2) Read or tell information. Do pages 66-78 or what you can cover. Discuss. **END**	**Day 2** *Writing and Spelling Road to Reading and Thinking* (1) Do your daily assignments for *WSRRT.* **Day 3** *Writing and Spelling Road to Reading and Thinking* (1) Do your daily assignments for *WSRRT.* **Day 4** *Writing and Spelling Road to Reading and Thinking* (1) Do your daily assignments for *WSRRT.*	**Day 2** *What Is Voice?* (1) Review **Day 4-5** Use this time to review anything from lesson 1.

On day 5 review any subject in Lesson 1 that needs a better understanding.

Continue the process with Lesson 2. See the *Road Map and Route Catalogue.*

Week 2 | **Month 2**
Lesson 2
Day 1
"The Chosen People"
(1) Music, Prayer, MV.
(2) Read and discuss.

Table of Contents

"God
WitH
Us"

Teacher Section

"Sing unto Him, sing psalms unto Him:
talk ye of all His wondrous works."
Psalm 105:2

INSTRUCTIONS
For the Teacher

Step 1

Study the Bible Lesson and begin to memorize the Memory Verses. Familiarize Yourself with the Character Quality.

The student can answer the Bible Review Questions. See page 5. Use the Steps in Bible Study.

Bible Lesson

"God With Us" – Genesis 3:14-15; 12:1-3; Galatians 3:16; Genesis 49:10; Deuteronomy 18:17-19; II Samuel 7:12-17; Ezekiel 21:25-27; Luke 1:32; Isaiah 9:6-7; Psalm 45:1-8; 72:1-11; Isaiah 53; Zechariah 12:10; John 14:9; John 1:1-4; Matthew 1:23

Memory Verses

Matthew 1:23; Matthew 1:20-21; John 8:28; 6:57; 7:18; 8:50; Philippians 2:5-11

Character Quality

Love – an affection of the mind excited by beauty and worth of any kind, or by the qualities of an object; charity.

Antonyms – hate; detestableness; abomination; loathing; scorn; disdainfulness; selfishness

Character Quality Verse

I Corinthians 13:4-7 – *"Charity suffereth long, and is kind; charity envieth not; charity vaunteth not itself, is not puffed up,*

"Doth not behave itself unseemly, seeketh not her own, is not easily provoked, thinketh no evil;

"Rejoiceth not in iniquity, but rejoiceth in the truth;

"Beareth all things, believeth all things, hopeth all things, endureth all things."

Step 2

Understand How To/ And

A. Do the Spelling Cards so the student can begin to build his own spiritual dictionary.

B. Mark the Bible.

C. Evaluate Your Student's Character in relation to the character quality of **love**.

D. Familiarize Yourself With the Voice. Notice the Projects.

E. Study the Scripture References for "Voice."

F. Notice the Answer Key.

A. Spelling Cards
Spelling Lists

Voice Words Place II - III	Bible Words
differences	blessing
distinct	bruise
instrument	Emmanuel
larynx	enmity
membrane	forever
obstructions	head
peculiarity	heel
pharynx	Judah
pitch	kingdom
power	lawgiver
quality	**love**
stretched	peace
tone	Prophet
vibration	scepter
vocal cords	seed
windpipe	Shiloh
	throne
	woman

See the booklet *Spelling from the Scriptures* for instructions.

B. How to Mark the Bible

1. Copy the list of Bible texts in the back of the Bible on an empty page as a guide.

2. Go to the first text in the Bible and copy the next text beside it. Go to the next one and repeat the process until they are all chain referenced.

3. Have the student present the study to family and/or friends.

4. In each student lesson there is one or more sections that have a Bible marking study on the subject studied. If there is not make up your own.

C. Evaluate Your Student's Character

This section is for the purpose of helping the teacher know how to encourage the students in becoming more **loving**.

See page 7.

Place I = Grades 2-3-4
Place II = Grades 4-5-6
Place III = Grades 6-7-8

D. Familiarize Yourself With What is the Voice? – Notice the Projects

Projects

1. As a family, discuss how God's **love** is expressed through the voice.

2. Use the Scripture song you made the music for in the Music Lesson, practice speaking the words without singing, making sure the words are clear and correctly pronounced.

On Sabbath sing the Scripture song you made up as a family for your friends. Thank God for using you to express His **love** to others.

3. Have the student explain in a paper he writes, God's purpose through the voice.

4. Read "Excerpt for Vocal" and "Vocal Fact Sheet."

5. Practice responding to others with a cheerful voice.

E. Study the Scripture References for 'Voice'

Teacher do a study about the voice from the Scriptures before working on the lesson with the student.

F. Notice the Answer Key

The Answer Key for the student book is found on page 11.

Notes

Read the Lesson Aim.

Lesson Aim

This lesson is to give the student an understanding of what the voice is and what God's purpose for it is. Even if a person could speak *"with the tongues of men and of angels,"* it would be of no value without **love**.

Help the student to relate this to the character quality of **love** that God manifested in giving His Son to us. Learn how, by the correct use of your voice, God can manifest His **love** to the world.

God is **love**, and it is His nature to give. He gave Jesus to reveal His **love** both to men and to angels. Jesus is the outshining of God's character. Jesus is God's thoughts made audible.

"...So Christ set up His tabernacle in the midst of our human encampment. He pitched His tent by the side of the tents of men, that He might dwell among us, and make us familiar with His divine character and life. *The word became flesh, and tabernacled among us and we beheld his glory, glory as of the Only*

Begotten of the father, full of grace and truth" (John 1:14)."*

The Word of God is what gives light and life to the fallen world. The voice is the means God gave to man to express God's word and **love** to a fallen world.

We can participate with God by letting Him use us to make His thoughts audible through our voice. We can express our **love** to Him and to others by speaking and singing God's word correctly.

The human voice exceeds every musical instrument. "Vocal music is one of God's gifts to men, an instrument that cannot be surpassed or equaled when God's **love** abounds in the soul."**

Notes

*The Desire of Ages 23-24
**The Voice in Speech and Song 425

Step 4

Prepare to begin the Voice Lesson.

To Begin the Voice Lesson

As an introduction to the lesson, read the story, "An Incident"

Step 5

Begin the Voice lesson. Cover only what can be understood by your student. Make the lessons a family project by all being involved in part or all of the lesson. These lessons are designed for the whole family.

Steps in Bible Study

1. Prayer

2. Read the verses/meditate/memorize.

3. Look up key words in *Strong's Concordance* and find their meaning in the Hebrew or Greek dictionary in the back of that book.

4. Cross reference (marginal reference) with other Bible texts. An excellent study tool is *The Treasury of Scripture Knowledge*.

5. Use Bible custom books for more information on the times.

6. Write a summary of what you have learned from those verses.

7. Mark key thoughts in the margin of your Bible.

8. Share your study with others to reinforce the lessons you have learned.

Review Questions

1. What were the circumstances under which the first promise of a Redeemer was given? (Genesis 3:14-15)

2. What promise was made to Abraham, and what did it mean? (Genesis 12:1-3; Galatians 3:16)

3. Through what tribe of Israel was the Messiah to come? (Genesis 49:10)

4. What promise was given through Moses? (Deuteronomy 18:17-19)

5. Through whom was the permanence of David's kingdom assured? (II Samuel 7:12-17; Ezekiel 21:25-27; Luke 1:32)

6. What exalted ideas concerning the Messiah were made prominent? (Isaiah 9:6, 7; Psalm 45:1-8; 72:1-11)

7. What also was foretold of His relation to sin? (Isaiah 53; Zechariah 12:10)

8. What is the significance of the name which John applies to Christ? (John 14:9; Matthew 1:23)

9. What important facts are stated of Him in John 1:1-4
        a.
        b.
        c.

10. As part of the great scheme of human redemption, what did the Word become? What is the meaning of the words *"became flesh?"* (Matthew 1:23)

Evaluating Your Child's Character

Check the appropriate box for your student's level of development,
or your own, as the case may be.

Maturing Nicely (MN), Needs Improvement (NI), Poorly Developed (PD), Absent (A)

Love

1. *"**Charity** suffereth long and is kind"* (I Corinthians 13:4). Does my child show a maturity of **love** that enables them to be kind while suffering from hunger, tiredness, or discomfort?

MN   NI   PD   A
❑   ❑   ❑   ❑

2. When the child encounters people with character deficiencies, is the child's reaction one of **loving** pity and concern instead of condemnation?

MN   NI   PD   A
❑   ❑   ❑   ❑

3. Does your child seem to **love** God more as a result of studying the material contained in the Bible?

MN   NI   PD   A
❑   ❑   ❑   ❑

4. *"**Charity**...vaunteth not itself; is not puffed up."* Does the child refrain from comparing himself with others? Do they make comments like "I can read better than _____ ."

MN   NI   PD   A
❑   ❑   ❑   ❑

5. *"**Charity**...seeketh not her own."* Is the child willing for others to have the best or the most of desirable things?

MN   NI   PD   A
❑   ❑   ❑   ❑

6. *"**Love** your enemies."* Does the child initiate reconciliation with or do kind things for those who have hard feelings toward him or who have treated him unfairly?

MN   NI   PD   A
❑   ❑   ❑   ❑

7. *"**Love** covers a multitude of sins."* Is the child eager to tell you about the failures of others or do they **lovingly** shield others from exposure where possible to do so with integrity?

MN   NI   PD   A
❑   ❑   ❑   ❑

8. *"**Charity**...thinketh no evil."* Is the child unsuspecting, ever placing the most favorable construction upon the motives and acts of others?

MN   NI   PD   A
❑   ❑   ❑   ❑

Excerpt for Vocal

"The human voice is a precious gift of God; it is a power for good, and the Lord wants His servants to preserve its pathos and melody. The voice should be cultivated so as to promote its musical quality, that it may fall pleasantly upon their ear and impress the heart." (*Evangelism* 667-668)

"As a sacred trust the voice should be used to honor God....The gospel of Christ is to be proclaimed by the voice....It should ever be used in God's service." (R H 9/12/1899)

Your voice, your influence, your time—all these are gifts from God and are to be used in winning souls to Christ." This should ever be our motive and purpose.

"Those who abide in Jesus will be happy, cheerful, and joyful in God. A subdued gentleness will mark the voice, reverence for spiritual and eternal things will be expressed in the actions, and music, joyful music, will echo from the lips; for it was wafter [conveyed] from the throne of God." (4T 626)

"**Love** illuminates the countenance and subdues the voice; it refines and elevates the entire man." (*4 Testimonies* 559-560)

THE HUMAN VOICE CAN SING PRAISES TO GOD

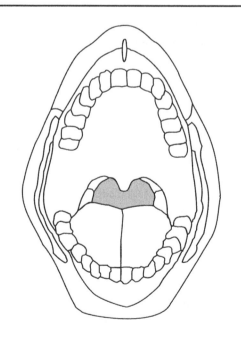

Vocal Fact Sheet

What is the voice? The voice is a <u>distinguishable</u> feature of someone or something. It is an expression of the giver, the means of transfer of thought. There are no two voices alike. The voice is a means of <u>identification</u>. Why, even the birds have a unique voice all their own. Every robin has a different voice from every other robin.

Because our voices are uniquely different, no one can express God's thoughts the way we can.

God has given us a talent called the voice. It is our duty to Him to cultivate that talent that we may give sounds and words of **praise** to others, and draw them to God.

As we cultivate our voice and speaking mannerisms, while maintaining a living connection with God, our voices and characters will become refined.

Refine – To improve in accuracy, delicacy, or anything that constitutes excellence. To become pure.

As we improve our voices, they will become melodious. Our voices, even as we speak, should have a musical quality about them. The voice should be pleasing to the ear.

As we express God's **love** through our voices, our manner should be the same as Jesus would have had.

God's thoughts are the thinking of His mind. Jesus' purpose for coming to this earth was to reveal God both to men and to angels, to make God's thoughts audible to men. It is to be our purpose also, to reveal God's thoughts through our voices.

> As we improve our voices, they will become melodious.

> As we express God's **love** through our voices, our manner should be the same as Jesus would have had.

An Incident

When I was a child, I sought, and I believed found, the dear Saviour. I was very happy, and wanted all my playmates to become Christians. But, alas! I did not always do right; and I fear that I sometimes stood in their way.

One day I asked my cousin if she would seek Jesus. She wanted to be good, but thought Christians were not all as good as they should be, and that there was not much difference between a Christian and one who was not. Said she, "Don't be angry with me, but I want to tell you that I have sometimes heard you speak unkindly to your sister."

She had, then, been watching me very closely; and my unguarded words had led her to distrust me as a Christian. I could not lead her to Christ. She grew up a proud woman. Since then, when I have heard children who profess religion use unkind words to playmates, brothers, sisters, or parents, I have thought of that incident in my boyhood days, and wondered if the result would be equally sad.

Remember, children, that if you are trying to be Christians, you will be watched very closely, to see if you err by word, act, or look. And, if you do wrong, they may not tell you of it, as my cousin did me, but, perhaps, will say to others, "I don't believe he is as good as he pretends to be, after all, or he would not be so ill-natured to his parents and play mates. If he is a Christian, I don't want to be one." Children, be careful of your words that they are always **loving**.

Answer Key

Page 8

1. Praise God
   Tell others of His wonderful **love**

2. Windpipe (Adam's Apple)

3. Vocal cords

4. Muscles, reed, air

5. Reed and stringed instruments.
   It is like a reed instrument since it
   requires air to operate it; and it is
   like a stringed instrument since the
   cords being tightened and loosened
   change the pitch.

6. No

7. Size of larynx
   Pharynx
   Size of sphenoid bone
   Thickness of cheekbone

8. Lack of free passage between the
   back part of the nasal cavity
   and the pharynx

9. Music of a life in harmony with
   God's law of **love**

Notes

"God With Us"

"Christ sought to teach the grand truth
so needful for us to learn,
that God is always with us,
an inmate of every dwelling,
that He is acquainted
with every action performed on earth.
He knows the thoughts that are framed in the mind
and endorsed by the soul.
He hears every word
that falls from the lips of human beings.
He is walking and working in the midst
of all our transactions in life.
He knows every plan,
and He measures every method."

My Life Today 290

Gardening Sheet

Lesson __One__   Subject __Voice__

Title __"What is the Voice?"__

In Season	Out of Season

(This is for "In Season" and "Out of Season.")

1. Make a list of voice terms for the garden.

2. Go on a treasure hunt finding the voice in the garden. (Examples: Adam's apple [apple tree], breath [wind], windpipe [hoses]).

3. Make spiritual parallels to the Bible Lesson or the character quality of **love**. (Example: Because Adam **loved** Eve more than he **loved** God he said yes to eating of the fruit when he should have said no. Which **love** was the pure kind of **love**—the **love** for Eve or God?)

Discuss what the character quality means and what it has to do with the garden?

Why should God have all of our **love**?

If He does how should we act in the garden when we are asked to pull weeds, water it, or pick beans?

Student Section

"...Let me see thy countenance,
let me hear thy voice;
for sweet is thy voice,
and thy countenance is comely."
Song of Solomon 2:14

What is the Voice?

  ## Research

The Human Voice

The human voice is a living musical instrument. It was created to praise God and to tell others of His wonderful **love**.

Sing and Talk

"Sing unto Him, sing psalms unto Him: talk ye of all His wondrous works."

Psalm 105:2

The Holy Spirit Can Inspire Our Utterances

Vocal Cords

The musical instrument of the body is located in the windpipe at the point called the "Adam's Apple." It is operated by the breath passing over the vocal cords as it rises from the lungs. This can remind us how the Spirit, also called breath in the Bible, is to inspire our words. The vocal cords consist of extensions of thin membrane from the sides of the windpipe. Muscles can tighten or loosen this membrane, making it vibrate like a reed as the air passes over it. The human musical instrument is like a combination of both a reed instrument and a stringed instrument. It is like a reed instrument since it requires air to operate it; and it is like a stringed instrument since the cords being loosened and tightened change the pitch.

Training

Our voice is the result of a complex arrangement of structures and tissues. In order to bring it to a state of perfection, much effort and time must necessarily be spent. It is not enough to have a sweet-toned piano or a delicately strung violin in the house; one must know how to use it. So with the voice. Nature has endowed us with a beautiful pipe organ; but it requires training to obtain sweet tones from it. We must have *"God with us,"* dwelling in our hearts and minds in order to have the kind of **loving** and spiritually powerful voice that God meant for each of us to have.

The voice is capable of being improved, the same as the mind or any other gift of nature. God desires for us to have beautiful voices and characters.

> "Let me see
> thy countenance,
> let me hear thy voice;
> for sweet is thy voice,
> and thy countenance
> is comely."
>
> Song of Solomon 2:14

We can recognize the voice of a friend from whom we have been separated for years by the voice's pitch, power, and tone,.

Quality

Every voice has a peculiar quality, an individuality, that cannot be changed. This is distinct from the pitch, or power, of the tone; it is distinct from the sweetness, richness, mellowness, or harshness, as such; it is simply the individuality. By it we recognize the voice of a friend from whom we have been separated for years. This peculiarity of tone is always present. It can remind us about the peculiar quality of God's *"still small voice,"* and how important it is that we become familiar enough with it to be able to tell the difference between it and the voice of self or the world.

Vibrations

You may ask, "what causes this peculiarity of tone in a person's voice?" It results from a combination of natural causes. In one person the vocal cords may be thick and short. This arrangement produces a different tone from one in which the vocal cords are thin, broad, and long, just as a thick, short wire stretched between two points produces a tone differing from the vibration of a fine, long wire. The differences in voices are only differences in the number and character of vibrations.

The differences in the vibrations of voices can remind us of the different way each soul vibrates in response to the Holy Spirit. Our souls are like harps which are to be tuned to God, and yet the unique experience of each person enables them to proclaim God's **loving** character in a different way than anyone else. What a beautiful symphony there will be when all of God's people come together in the courts above and sing their part in the song of God's **love**.

"And I heard
a voice from Heaven,
as the voice
of many waters,
and as the voice
of a great thunder:
and I heard the voice
of Harpers Harping
with their Harps:
And they sung
as it were
a new song
before the throne...."

Revelation 14:2-3

Differences

Many causes tend to modify the vibration, and hence alter the voice. No two individuals have the same sized larynx (the upper part of the windpipe that contains the vocal cords) or pharynx (the space behind the mouth into which the nostrils, gullet, and windpipe open), and more than any two faces are exactly alike. In one the pharynx may be long; in another it may be broad. Some people have a high arch in the roof of their mouth; in others, it is low and flat. All these conditions affect the tone of the voice in speaking and singing.

There are other conditions, also, that have an important bearing upon the quality of tones produced by the vocal organs. Just back of the mouth is a bone called the "sphenoid bone." The central portion of this bone is not solid, but hollow, and is made up of many little cells. These vary considerably in size and form in different individuals. In the cheekbones, also, are large spaces (cavities). In all cases, these cavities in the bones are lined with a mucous membrane. As the tones produced by the vocal cords strike against these different hollow bones, the number of vibrations is increased, and their character is modified by the degree of thickness of the bone and the size of the cells within. By striking a solid body, a dull sound is produced; but striking a hollow body results in a different note. The same principle holds good in the formation of vocal tones. It can remind us how a solid faith will ring differently than a hollow pretense.

Illustrations

Side view of the head and neck showing the mouth, the pharynx and the side wall of the nasal cavity.

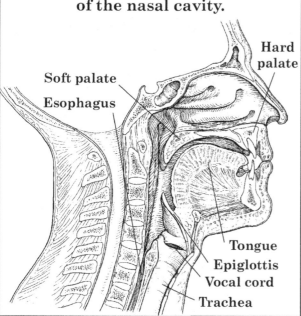

Hard palate

Soft palate

Esophagus

Tongue
Epiglottis
Vocal cord
Trachea

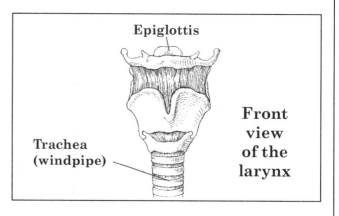

Epiglottis

Trachea (windpipe)

Front view of the larynx

Obstructions

If there is not a free passage between the back part of the nasal cavity and the pharynx, the voice is affected, and this gives rise to the so-called "nasal tone," or "talking through the nose." This condition often results from an inflamed condition of the lining membrane which causes too much mucous to be made. If the tonsils are very large, it is difficult either to talk or to sing with freedom.

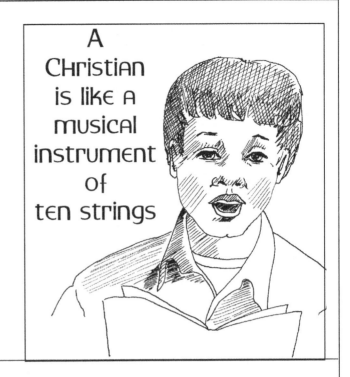

A Christian is like a musical instrument of ten strings

A Talent

Thus we see that quality of tone depends upon many conditions; and that, with the exception of the last two conditions mentioned, we cannot change the structures that combine to produce a good voice. All cannot become equally good singers; but all can improve. All are not born with the natural talent of professional singers, any more than all possess the genius of Edison; but this should not discourage anyone. Real genius is a capacity for hard work, and a diligent determination to succeed. Continual striving brings success. Thankfully, all can:

"Make a joyful noise unto the Lord."
Psalm 100:1

If our voices leave something to be desired, this need not be so with our characters. A Christian is like a musical instrument of ten strings—with each of the Ten Commandments being a string or key. Maybe the sweet psalmist of Israel had this in mind when he wrote in Psalm 33:2, *"Praise the lord with ... an instrument of ten strings."* The sweetest music in all the world is the music of a life in harmony with God's law of **love**.*

"Praise the lord with.... an instrument of ten strings."
Psalm 33:2

*Adapted from F. M. Rossiter, M.D.

Reinforce

1. When singing or talking feel your throat to feel the vibrations of the vocal cord.

2. Look at reed and string musical instruments and realize the human voice is a musical instrument.

3. Listen to several different people speak and notice the pitch and tone of their voices.

4. Note the differences in how each member of your family speaks.

6. Have you ever had a cold and sounded like you were talking through your nose? Demonstrate this for your teacher.

7. Read the poem, "The Voice."

Notice the difference in the tones in an adult and in a child.

Remind

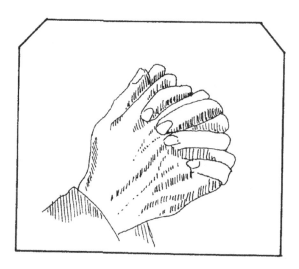

1. Think before speaking. Make sure the Holy Spirit is directing your thoughts and words.

2. When tying string around a package be reminded that the vocal cords change the pitch of the human voice. It can depend on if they are loose or tight.

3. As you play the piano think how you need to learn how to use it, just like you need to learn how to use the human voice.

4. If you see different sizes of wire consider how the vocal cords may be thick or thin.

5. Remember, our souls are like harps which are to be tuned to God.

6. Let our voices always speak in tones of **love**.

THE VOICE

Oh the music and the beauty
    Of a soft and gentle voice!
How it fills the soul with sunshine!
    How it makes the heart rejoice!
How the merry laugh of childhood
    Seems to banish every care,
As it echoes through the wildwood,
    In and out and everywhere!

Ah! 'tis sweeter than the music
    Of earth's famous organs grand,
Than the singing of the worldly
    And their rude discordant band.
Oh the music and the beauty
    Of a soft and gentle voice!
How it fills the soul with sunshine!
    How it makes the heart rejoice!

—Adapted from Mrs. L.D. Avery-Suttle

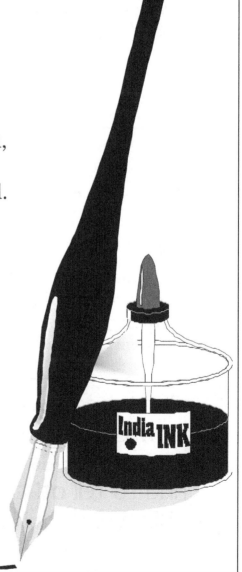

Review

Place II- III

1. What are two important uses for the voice?

2. Where is the musical instrument of the human body located?

3. What are the membranes extending from the sides of the windpipe called?

4. __ __ __ __ __ __ __ can tighten or loosen this membrane, making it vibrate like a __ __ __ __ as the __ __ __ passes over it.

5. The human voice is like a combination of two musical instruments. What are they? How is the voice like each of them?

6. Can all become equally good singers if they just practice enough?

7. List four things about a person's body that affect the tone of their voice.

(1)_____

(2) _____

(3) _____

(4) _____

8. What causes a "nasal tone" of voice?

9. What is the sweetest music in all the world?

THE HUMAN VOICE WAS CREATED to praise God and to tell others of His wonderful **love.**

Outline of School Program

Age	Grade	Program
Birth through Age 7	Babies Kindergarten and Pre-school	*Family Bible Lessons* (This includes: Bible, Science–Nature, and Character)
Age 8	First Grade	*Family Bible Lessons* (This includes: Bible, Science–Nature, and Character) + Language Program (*Writing and Spelling Road to Reading and Thinking* [WSRRT])
Age 9-14 or 15	Second through Eighth Grade	*The Desire of all Nations* (This includes: Health, Mathematics, Music, Science–Nature, History/Geography/Prophecy, Language, and Voice–Speech) + Continue using WSRRT
Ages 15 or 16-19	Ninth through Twelfth Grade	9 – *Cross and Its Shadow I** + Appropriate Academic Books 10 – *Cross and Its Shadow II** + Appropriate Academic Books 11 – *Daniel the Prophet** + Appropriate Academic Books 12 – *The Seer of Patmos** (Revelation) + Appropriate Academic Books *or you could continue using *The Desire of Ages*
Ages 20-25	College	Apprenticeship

Made in the USA
Monee, IL
21 August 2022

11941386R00024